GALE
CENGAGE Learning

Literary Newsmakers for Students, Volume 1

Project Editor
Anne Marie Hacht

Editorial
Sara Constantakis and Ira Mark Milne

Rights Acquisition and Management
Margaret Chamberlain-Gaston and Robyn Young

Manufacturing
Drew Kalasky

Imaging
Lezlie Light, Mike Logusz, and Kelly Quin

Product Design
Pamela A. E. Galbreath

Vendor Administration
Civie Green

Product Manager
Meggin Condino

copyright notices, the acknowledgments constitute an extension of the copyright notice.

While every effort has been made to ensure the reliability of the information presented in this publication, Gale, an imprint of Cengage Learning does not guarantee the accuracy of the data contained herein. Gale, an imprint of Cengage Learning accepts no payment for listing; and inclusion in the publication of any organization, agency, institution, publication, service, or individual does not imply endorsement of the editors or publisher. Errors brought to the attention of the publisher and verified to the satisfaction of the publisher will be corrected in future editions.

ISBN 13: 978-1-4144-0282-6
ISBN 10: 1-4144-0281-3
ISSN: 1559-9639

This title is also available as an e-book
ISBN-13: 978-1-4144-2930-4, ISBN-10: 1-4144-2930-4
Contact your Gale, an imprint of Cengage Learning representative for ordering information.

Printed in the United States of America
10 9 8 7 6 5 4 3 2 1

The Kite Runner

KHALED HOSSEINI

2003

INTRODUCTION

The Kite Runner by Khaled Hosseini was published in 2003. Initially published by Riverhead Books, an imprint of Penguin, *The Kite Runner* was said to be the first novel written in English by an Afghan writer, and the book appeared on many book club reading lists. The novel is set in Afghanistan from the late 1970s to 1981 and the start of the Soviet occupation, then in the Afghan community in Fremont, California from the 1980s to the early

2000s, and finally in contemporary Afghanistan during the Taliban regime.

The Kite Runner is the story of strained family relationships between a father and a son, and between two brothers, how they deal with guilt and forgiveness, and how they weather the political and social transformations of Afghanistan from the 1970s to 2001. *The Kite Runner* opens in 2001. The adult narrator, Amir, lives in San Francisco and is contemplating his past, thinking about a boyhood friend whom he has betrayed. The action of the story then moves backward in time to the narrator's early life in Kabul, Afghanistan, where he is the only child of a privileged merchant. Amir's closest friend is his playmate and servant Hassan, a poor illiterate boy who is a member of the Hazara ethnic minority. *The Kite Runner*, a coming-of-age novel, deals with the themes of identity, loyalty, courage, and deception. As the protagonist Amir grows to adulthood, he must come to terms with his past wrongs and adjust to a new culture after leaving Afghanistan for the United States.

The novel sets the interpersonal drama of the characters against the backdrop of the modern history of Afghanistan, sketching the political and economic toll of the instability of various regimes in Afghanistan; from the end of the monarchy to the Soviet-backed government of the 1980s to the fundamentalist Taliban government of the 1990s. The action closes soon after the fall of the Taliban and alludes to the rise of Hamid Karzai as leader of a new Afghan government in the wake of the events of September 11, 2001.

AUTHOR BIOGRAPHY

Khaled Hosseini was born in 1965 in Kabul, Afghanistan, the setting of much of the action in *The Kite Runner*. Hosseini and his family moved to Paris in 1976, then immigrated to the United States in 1980 as refugees with political asylum. Hosseini's parents, a former diplomat and a teacher, settled in San Jose, California, where they subsisted on welfare until his father, working odd jobs, managed to independently support the family. Hosseini received a biology degree in 1988 from Santa Clara University and a medical degree from the University of California, San Diego in 1993. As of 2005, he is a practicing physician, specializing in internal medicine in Northern California.

Hosseini published several stories before writing his first novel, *The Kite Runner*, which was based on an earlier short story of the same title. As a doctor with an active practice and many patients, Hosseini struggled to find time to expand the story, so he wrote the novel piecemeal in the early morning hours. Hosseini contends that treating patients made him a keen observer of people and the ways they express themselves, both verbally and nonverbally.

In 2004, Hosseini was selected by the Young Adult Library Services Association to receive an Alex Award, an honor given to the authors of the ten best adult books for teenagers published in the previous year. Also in 2004, he was given the Original Voices award by the Borders Group, and *The Kite Runner* was nominated for a Pushcart Prize.

His next novel, entitled *Dreaming in Titanic City*, is slated for publication in 2006.

PLOT SUMMARY

Chapters 1-5

The Kite Runner opens in December 2001. The narrator, Amir, meditates on the past, recalling a walk in San Francisco's Golden Gate Park, and alludes to a more distant moment of crisis in 1976. The narrator considers the way that the past has a way of returning despite one's efforts to forget it. He mentions the names of several characters slated to appear in later chapters. After this opening, the novel uses a flashback, a device through which the narrator tells about events that happened before the present action of the story. This flashback lasts for many chapters, returning the reader, near the end of the novel, to 2001, the time in which the first chapter is set. The first five chapters sketch the details of Amir's childhood in Kabul, his daily life with his friend and servant Hassan in his father's large house, and his burgeoning interest in literature. Hassan and his father live on Amir's father's property in a separate servant's house. They are members of a minority ethnic group in Afghanistan known as the Hazara. Victims of casual discrimination by the privileged classes, the Hazara in *The Kite Runner* are derided for their appearance and generally live as second-class citizens. However, Hassan and his father Ali, servants in Baba's household, are treated fairly well as members of the family. Ali has known Baba for decades and Hassan and Amir, despite their differences in ethnicity and status, are constant playmates.

As if to further emphasize the differences between them, Hassan has a birth defect, a harelip, which gives him the appearance of constantly smiling. The reader sees the relationship between the young Amir and Hassan in several crucial scenes. The most important of these depicts an encounter between the two friends and a group of older bullies led by Assef, a half-German, half-Afghan boy who accuses Amir of being a traitor to the Pashtun ethnicity by playing with a Hazara boy. While Amir is paralyzed with fear, Hassan ignores the racist insults and drives the bullies away by threatening them with his slingshot. Assef and his minions retreat, but not before Assef threatens revenge.

The novel details the increasingly turbulent political developments in Afghanistan. As Amir and Hassan grow up, dreaming of being Rostan and Sohrab, the heroes of the Afghan heroic legend the *Shahnammah*, the events of history invade their world of stories and play. Amir and Hassan get a taste of how politics can affect daily life when they hear gunfire in the streets. Although Ali tells the boys that it is only the sound of fireworks, these sounds foreshadow, or look ahead to, the overthrow of the monarchy by a military coup. Meanwhile, Amir and Hassan continue to play together, but Amir often feels jealous of the attention that Hassan receives from Baba, who treats Hassan less like a servant than like a family member. Indeed, for Hassan's birthday, Baba pays a surgeon to perform an operation to correct his harelip. As Hassan is healing from his surgery, Amir sees him gingerly smile with his new mouth, an observation that foreshadows tragic events to come.

Chapters 6-7

The narrator meditates on the fun times Amir and Hassan enjoy during the wintertime and describes the events leading up to the 1975 kite tournament in Kabul. Amir describes the annual kite festival, the strategy of kite-fighting, and the importance of "kite runners" like Hassan, who retrieve the kites cut down by the razor-sharp strings of victorious kites as the surviving competitors become fewer and fewer. These detailed descriptions of the practice and strategies of kite-fighting and kite-running lead into a flashback that showcases Hassan's uncanny talent at running down fallen kites. Encouraged by his father, Amir decides to compete seriously in the kite-fighting competition, in part because he genuinely enjoys the sport, but mostly because he hopes to earn his father's admiration by winning the tournament.

On the morning of the kite tournament, Hassan relates a strange dream he has had in which he and Amir swim out into Ghargha Lake, which is said to be inhabited by a terrible monster. In this dream they swim out and return unharmed, despite the dozens of onlookers on the shore warning them to return. Although Amir, irritable from a restless night's sleep, dismisses the dream, it proves prophetic. The narration shows the reader the excitement and festivity of the streets on the day of the kite tournament as well as the seriousness of the competitors. Amir's extreme nervousness is compounded by the knowledge that his father is finally supporting him and plans to watch the tournament from his rooftop. Tensions between father and son are so strained that Amir actually wonders whether, if he loses, his father might take pleasure in his defeat. Nevertheless, Amir performs admirably, making many impressive tactical maneuvers until his and another kite are the only two remaining. Amir cuts the last kite out of the sky and sees his father on the roof cheering for him. He also shares the moment of victory with Hassan, who promises to run after the last defeated kite. Hassan is eager to help his friend by retrieving the prize: "For you a thousand times over!" Hassan finds the fallen kite, but is chased by some other boys. Amir follows some noises to an alley off the bazaar where, undetected himself, he discovers a horrific scene: Assef, Kamal, and Wali threaten to take the kite from Hassan; Hassan, unable to fight them off, is raped by Assef while Assef's friends hold him down. Rather than step in and fight Hassan's attackers, Amir freezes, remains hidden, and eventually runs away in fear. After the rape, Hassan finds Amir in the street and they return home with the kite without discussing the attack at all, although Hassan is visibly distraught. Amir returns home to a hero's welcome from his father and his father's friends.

Chapters 8-9

Hassan becomes extremely remote, performing his household duties invisibly and avoiding Amir entirely. Neither Amir nor Hassan reveal to Baba what has happened; Amir tries to avoid thinking of his failure to protect his friend. Against the backdrop of this guilt, Amir takes advantage of the opportunity to enjoy his father's company, now that his father is publicly and unreservedly proud of his accomplishment in the kite tournament. Still, Amir harbors some jealousy when Baba expresses concern for Hassan after noticing that the other boy is withdrawn. Ali reports that Hassan has been ill. Amir's newfound closeness with his father proves tenuous when Amir, unable to face his guilt about Hassan, suggests that Baba look for new servants to replace Ali and Hassan. Baba angrily rejects the suggestion, insisting that they are not just servants but part of the family. Baba throws a massive celebration in honor of Amir's thirteenth birthday in the summer of 1976, during which Amir is forced to exchange pleasantries with Assef, who comes to the party accompanied by his parents and bearing a peculiar gift: a biography of Hitler. Unable to bear the festivities, Amir retreats to a quiet place where Rahim Khan finds him, talks to him, and gives him a special gift—a notebook in which to write his stories.

After the party, Amir's room is piled with

unsolicited tributes of both gifts and cash. Overwhelmed with gifts and praise and haunted by guilt, he takes some of the money and a brand new watch and plants them in Hassan's bed. Unable to bear the false implication that Hassan has stolen from Amir and Baba, Ali and Hassan leave the house in Kabul. While Amir is aware that he is causing great pain to others, including his father who seems devastated by their departure, he does nothing to correct the falsehood he created.

Chapters 10-13

Taking place six years later, these chapters begin with the traumatic political transition to the Soviet-backed Communist regime of Afghanistan during the 1980s and explain Amir and Baba's declining fortunes under the new order. In 1981, Amir and his father are compelled to leave everything behind and flee the country for Peshawar, Pakistan inside the tank of a fuel truck, with dozens of other refugees. During this escape, Baba again demonstrates the fearlessness for which he is admired by risking his life to save a woman from rape by a Russian soldier at a checkpoint.

After a sojourn in Pakistan, Amir and his father go to Fremont, California, an area where many other Afghan immigrants have settled. There they have a modest life, living in small apartments. Baba works, Amir studies, and they go to the Saturday flea market to sell their wares alongside other Afghan immigrants. Baba, unable to adjust to life in the United States, works at a gas station so that Amir can go to school and enter college. Meanwhile, Amir helps to smooth over his father's conflicts with American culture and enjoys his remoteness from a painful past. He falls in love with a young Afghan woman named Soraya Taheri, whom he gets to know at the Saturday swap meets. He asks Baba to "go *khastegari*" for him, to ask Soraya's father for her hand in marriage. Meanwhile, Baba, a lifelong smoker, is diagnosed with cancer. Turning down chemotherapy and radiation, he forbids Amir to speak of his illness. Though his cancer has spread alarmingly, he helps Amir perform the traditional Afghan courtship and engagement ceremonies. When Soraya and her father agree to the union, the couple forgoes the traditional long engagement period, knowing that Baba does not have long to live. Baba dies one month after they are married. Amir becomes acquainted with his wife's family and learns of disagreements between Soraya and her father, particularly relating to the double standards of Afghan gender politics. Amir and Soraya move to a new apartment. Amir works on his writing while Soraya studies to become a teacher. In 1989, just after the Soviets leave Afghanistan, Amir publishes his first novel, a story of a father and son in Kabul. The couple's happiness is spoiled only by their discovery that they cannot conceive a child.

Chapters 14-16

Amir and Soraya buy a house in San

Francisco. In 2001, Amir gets a call from Baba's old friend Rahim Khan, who is ill and living in Pakistan. Disturbed by memories of the past he has tried to forget, Amir plans his trip to Pakistan to see him. He considers Rahim Khan's suggestion that by coming to Pakistan he may have a chance to redeem himself. Arriving in Peshawar, Amir goes immediately to the shabby room where a frail and sickly Rahim Khan is staying in the city's Afghan Town. In his account of the current state of affairs in Afghanistan, Rahim Khan describes the violence and factionalism of the Northern Alliance rule from 1992 until 1996. He explains how Afghans saw the 1996 takeover by the Taliban as a harbinger of peace and order, little knowing the repression the Taliban would bring. Rahim Khan tells Amir that he is dying and tells him that Hassan, Amir's boyhood friend and servant, lived with him in Kabul in Baba's old house.

Told from the point of view of Rahim Khan—the only chapter not from Amir's point of view—Chapter 16 is another extended flashback that recounts Rahim Khan's life in Kabul after Amir and Baba went into exile. Living by himself in Baba's house, Rahim Khan becomes lonely, as more and more of his friends flee the country. In the late 1980s, during the era of the Soviet-backed government, Rahim Khan goes to a small village in Hazajarat to seek out Hassan and to ask him to bring his young wife Farzana back to Kabul to live with him and to help take care of the house. Hassan agrees to the arrangement, settling with Farzana in the old servants'house of his boyhood. Hassan's long-lost mother Sanaubar, who ran away in 1964, reappears, abused and starving. After nursing Sanaubar back to relative health, Hassan and Farzana have a baby boy whom they name Sohrab after the Afghan heroic tale of Rostam and Sohrab. In 1995, when Sohrab is four years old, Sanaubar dies. During the infighting and instability of the Northern Alliance period, when Kabul is sectioned off and ruled by competing groups, the little family nevertheless maintains a peaceful haven amid the chaos. Young Sohrab learns to read and attends the winter kite tournament with his father Hassan. The 1996 Taliban takeover leads to repression and violence: the Taliban bans Kabul's traditional kite tournament and massacres the Hazara population of Mazar-e-Sharif.

Chapters 17-24

Following Rahim Khan's first-person account, he hands Amir a letter from Hassan and a photograph of Hassan as a young man. After reading it, Amir learns that Hassan and his wife have been executed by the Taliban. The fate of their young son Sohrab is unknown. Furthermore, Rahim Khan reveals, Hassan is not only Amir's former servant and friend, but his half brother, the offspring of Amir's father and Hassan's mother Sanaubar. Stunned by these revelations, Amir thinks about his father's decades-long deception and tries to absorb the fact that Hassan was his brother all along. Though initially overcome by fear, Amir decides to travel to Afghanistan to rescue Hassan's son Sohrab.

Car sick and feeling estranged from the country of his childhood, Amir re-enters Afghanistan, led by his tough-talking guide and driver, Farid. Armed with Afghani currency and a picture of Sohrab and Hassan, Amir also wears a false beard to shield him from the Taliban's prying eyes. Farid, suspicious of his apparently pampered "American" passenger, updates Amir about the current state of affairs in his home country and awakens Amir to the fact that his class privilege has always shielded him from the reality of life as experienced by most Afghans. Despite Farid's initial suspicion of Amir's motives, he decides to help Amir find and rescue Sohrab. Farid drives Amir from Jalalabad, past villages destroyed by the Taliban to the city of Kabul, which, Farid informs him, is much changed. Despite this warning, Amir is shocked when they enter the city and see the signs of destruction and poverty everywhere. Amir has a frightening close encounter with the Taliban who roam the streets in pickup trucks looking for violations of the strict Shari'a law. A beggar who was a former university professor tells Amir the location of the orphanage where he hopes to find Sohrab. From Zaman, a beleaguered orphanage director, Amir and Farid learn that Sohrab has been taken away by a powerful Taliban official who is most likely sexually abusing the boy. Zaman tells them they can find the official at a soccer exhibition. Farid and Amir go to the soccer stadium, where, with the rest of the crowd, they witness a double execution by stoning. Following Shari'a law, the Taliban have sentenced a man and a woman to death for adultery. Before Amir's horrified gaze, a tall charismatic man in white robes appears, raising his arms in response to the roaring crowd, and personally stones the offenders to death. The Taliban official who throws the stones turns out to be the man the orphanage director described. Frightened and disgusted by what they have just seen, Amir and Farid nevertheless arrange to visit this official.

At the official's compound, Amir discovers that the high-ranking Talib is none other than Assef, Hassan's attacker from decades before. Assef behaves erratically, and Amir observes the marks of a heroin addiction on his arms. Assef boasts about his participation in the 1998 massacre of Hazara people in Mazar-e-Sharif, announcing that the violence was ordained by God. Assef calls Sohrab into the room to meet Amir, and tells Amir he remembers him from their childhood in Kabul. Assef forces Sohrab, who is costumed like a dancing girl, to perform for Amir and his guards. Amir confronts Assef, demanding that he turn over Sohrab. Assef sends his guards out of the room and challenges Amir to fight for the right to take Sohrab away. A long, violent fight between Amir and Assef ends when Sohrab uses his slingshot to blind Assef. Amir and Sohrab manage to escape in Farid's waiting car. Amir's injuries from the battle are so grave that he passes out and remains unconscious for two days. He awakens in a hospital in Pakistan, where he thanks a shy and reserved Sohrab for saving his life with the slingshot. Days later, the search for the charity that was to have taken in

Sohrab turns out to be fruitless. Rahim Khan himself has disappeared, leaving for Amir only a letter and a key to a safe-deposit box.

Chapters 24-25

With no one else to take care of him, Sohrab accompanies Amir to Islamabad, where they go to escape Taliban spies who may be searching for them in Peshawar. Amir asks Sohrab if he would like to come to America to live with him and his wife. Sohrab agrees only when Amir promises never to place him in an orphanage. Amir calls Soraya to ask her to consent to the arrangement. She agrees, but a consultation with a U.S. Embassy official reveals bureaucratic obstacles. An immigration lawyer advises a new course of action, namely, to put Sohrab in a Pakistan orphanage for a year until he can be officially declared an orphan. When Sohrab learns of this plan, he attempts suicide. At the same time, Amir learns from Soraya that a relative who works for the Immigration and Nationalization Service has arranged for a humanitarian visa with which Sohrab can enter the United States immediately. Amir waits for the outcome of the emergency surgery that he prays will save Sohrab's life. In the urgency of the moment, Amir prays to God for the first time in fifteen years, experiencing a sudden renewal of his Muslim faith. Sohrab survives. After several days'vigil in the hospital, Amir tells Sohrab about the humanitarian visa. Sohrab decides to go to the United States, but his depression is so profound that he does not speak for a year. His silent remoteness persists for months—through the aftermath of September 11, 2001, including the Taliban's defeat and the emergence of Hamid Karzai. The novel closes at an Afghan community gathering in Fremont, California in 2002. Amir buys a traditional Afghan kite, complete with glass string, and flies it with Sohrab, eliciting a faint smile from Sohrab, who remembers flying kites with his father Hassan in the wintertime. When their kite cuts down a competitor's kite, Amir runs to retrieve the fallen kite for Sohrab, echoing the words of Hassan from decades before: "For you a thousand times over."

MEDIA ADAPTATIONS

- Simon and Schuster released the audio book version of *The Kite Runner* by Khaled Hosseini in 2003. The author reads the audio book version. In audio form, the novel runs twelve hours and spans eight cassette tapes or eleven CDs.

CHARACTERS

Ali

Ali is the lifelong servant of Baba's family. Stricken with polio as a child, Ali endures the ridicule of the local boys for his pronounced limp and gnarled appearance. Steadfastly loyal to Baba and Amir, Ali lives with his only child Hassan in a modest servant's house on Baba's property. Ali was abandoned by his wife Sanaubar, who ran away soon after giving birth to Hassan. He belongs to the marginalized Hazara ethnic group, which historically resided in the mountainous Hazajarat region of Afghanistan. Despite this, Ali is a proud man who rejects dishonor and leaves Baba's household rather than live with the shame of his son being thought a thief.

Amir

Amir is the protagonist of *The Kite Runner*. Born into a privileged Pashtun family, Amir grows up in Kabul, Afghanistan raised by his father. His mother died in childbirth. As a boy, Amir is bookish, thoughtful, and unathletic. An introverted thinker, he prefers to write stories in his notebook rather than play soccer, much to his father's chagrin. Amir indulges in a recurrent fantasy of a warmer understanding with his father and is strongly motivated by the wish to make this fantasy a reality

—ultimately with tragic results. Constantly trying to earn his father's approval, Amir struggles for every scrap of his father's attention. He becomes jealous when his father pays more attention to Hassan, the son of the family servant Ali. Still, Amir is close to his servant and playmate Hassan. They spend entire days together, especially in the wintertime, and carve their names in a tree behind the house. Torn between affection for his friend and his need for his father's love, Amir often takes advantage of Hassan's gullibility and illiteracy. Ironically, his propensity to trick Hassan—making up false stories he pretends to read out of his schoolbooks—inspires him to discover his future calling as a writer. After moving to the United States with his father, Amir becomes a student and later a writer. After marrying a young Afghan woman named Soraya Taheri, he publishes his first novel. However, his childhood betrayal of Hassan haunts his adult life, and he eventually travels back to Kabul in order to make things right.

Assef

An older bully who also comes from a privileged family, Assef is the tall, blond-haired son of a German mother and an Afghan father. Flanked by flunkies who assist him in his misdeeds, Assef is a racist with a fascistic streak. He admires Hitler, and even gives Amir a biography of Hitler as a birthday present. Assef believes Afghanistan should be "purified" of the Hazara ethnic group and kept for the dominant Pashtun ethnic group alone. After an encounter with Amir and Hassan in which Hassan forces Assef to retreat with his slingshot, Assef vows payback. Later, with the help of two flunkies, he gets his revenge by raping Hassan in an alley on the night of the annual kite-fighting contest. Assef frightens Amir with his apparently sadistic personality; even Assef's own parents are cowed in his presence as if they, too, fear him. Assef grows up to become a high-ranking official in the Taliban government, when he and Amir meet for a final time.

Baba

A stubborn, energetic man and a prosperous merchant, Amir's father is as well-respected for his commercial successes as for his philanthropic endeavors. A great host, Baba is given to grand gestures and excessive hospitality. After his wife died while giving birth to Amir, Baba finds it difficult to relate to a son who is so different from himself—introverted, tentative, and intellectual instead of outgoing, strong, and decisive. He observes with disgust that when Amir and Hassan get into scrapes with local boys, Hassan, not Amir, stands up to the bullies. Baba never remarried, preferring to surround himself with male friends and business associates in a house more often than not filled with guests. A Sunni Muslim and an ethical man, Baba counsels his son never to steal; yet he opposes organized religion and dismisses the warnings of the mullahs (religious teachers) who provide religious instruction in Amir's schools.

Despite his stern attitude toward his son, he is a loving father. When Baba and Amir move to California, Baba works at a gas station so Amir can complete his schooling. He proudly presents his son to the Taheri family as a prospective husband for their daughter Soraya, and in the end respects his son for who he has become.

Farid

A driver and guide introduced to Amir by Rahim Khan in Peshawar, Pakistan. Farid is a tough man who has lost several family members to Taliban violence. He drives Amir to Kabul to rescue Sohrab, Hassan's son. Suspicious of Amir at first, Farid eventually respects him for risking his life to save a boy he has never met. Although he has responsibilities, with a wife and small children, he chooses to help Amir on an honorable mission.

Farzana

A young Hazara woman, Farzana is Hassan's wife and Sohrab's mother. After living in Hazarajat, she and Hassan move to Kabul where they live with Rahim Khan in Amir and Baba's old house. When Hassan's mother Sanaubar appears after a decades-long absence, Farzana nurses the older woman back to health. When she gives birth to Sohrab, Sanaubar serves as her midwife. Farzana, along with Hassan, is shot and killed by the Taliban for being a Hazara in the wrong area of Kabul.

Hassan

The son of Ali, Hassan is also a servant at Baba's house and about the same age as Amir. Fiercely loyal, Hassan is Amir's constant companion. Although born with a harelip, he is unselfconscious and happy, known for his easy smile. Illiterate but endowed with a sharp native intelligence, Hassan is strong, athletic, and courageous. Incapable of deceit, he cannot tell when Amir is tricking him. His premier talent is running the kites in the annual winter kite tournament in Kabul. Kite runners chase the fallen kites that are the casualties of the contest. Hassan has an uncanny ability to sense where the kites will land. His innocent, trusting nature belies a perceptiveness about Amir's state of mind. For example, Hassan reassures Amir when Amir is nervous about his performance in the annual kite competition. After Hassan is raped by the bully Assef, Hassan knows Amir saw the attack and did nothing but never raises the subject. Instead, when Amir betrays him a second time by telling Baba that Hassan has stolen from them, Hassan apologizes as if he committed the crime. Hassan and Ali leave Kabul and return to the Hazajarat region where the Hazara people have historically resided, but Hassan never holds a grudge against Amir for his actions.

Kamal

One of Assef's companions who reluctantly helps Assef rape Hassan, Kamal later becomes the victim of a similar attack and dies as he and his father attempt to escape Afghanistan for Pakistan during the repressive Soviet-backed regime.

Rahim Khan

Baba's business associate, Rahim Khan frequently visits with Baba to discuss their common commercial interests, Afghan politics, and personal matters. As his best friend and advisor, Khan frequently steps in when friction between father and son creates misunderstandings. Khan encourages Amir's interest in writing by giving him a journal for his thirteenth birthday and sympathizes with the latter's desperate attempts to earn his father's approval. Khan is also the guardian of a serious family secret. After Amir and Baba leave Afghanistan, he lives in their house, hoping to return it to them once the political turmoil in Kabul comes to an end. Later, growing older and lonelier, Khan finds Hassan and brings the latter and his wife to live with him in Kabul. Khan becomes gravely ill and moves to Pakistan. He contacts the adult Amir in the United States, summons him to Pakistan, and relates to Amir the history of Hassan, his wife, and their young son.

Sohrab

The young son of Hassan and Farzana, born in Kabul, who survives his parents'execution by the Taliban. Sohrab is named after one of the heroes of the traditional Afghan heroic tale, the *Shahnammah*.

After his parents'death, Sohrab lands in an ill-equipped orphanage in Kabul, where the children are preyed upon by lecherous Taliban officials. After escaping from his abuser and going with Amir to Pakistan, Sohrab tries to commit suicide upon hearing he may have to return to an orphanage. When he awakes after emergency surgery, he tells Amir that he is too tired to live. Provided with a humanitarian visa, Sohrab can go to the United States to live with Amir and Soraya, where he lives in silence. He does not utter a word for the first year he is there.

General Iqbal Taheri

The father of Soraya, Amir's love interest, General Taheri is a dignified man well-known in the Afghan community in Northern California. Always clad in a worn, but well-made suit, General Taheri is too proud to work, viewing common work as a contradiction to his former importance in the Afghan government. He goes to the weekly flea market where he socializes with other Afghan immigrants who gather there every weekend, referring to his modest flea market trade as a "hobby" that allows him to keep in touch with friends. His wife and daughter tend their market stall while the General talks politics with their friends and neighbors. General Taheri hopes for the end of the Taliban regime and an offer to return to Kabul to take a post in a future Afghan government.

Khanum Taheri

Also known as Khala Jamila, Khanum Taheri is General Taheri's wife and Soraya's mother. Endowed with a bubbly personality and a streak of hypochondria, she frequently worries about her health or her family. Although she was once well-known in Kabul for her beautiful singing voice, her husband now forbids her to sing in public.

Soraya Taheri

Soraya is the daughter of the once-prominent General Taheri who had a great deal of influence in the government of the pre-Taliban Afghanistan. An intelligent, beautiful young woman, she adheres to the traditions of the patriarchal Afghan culture, despite her rebellious attitude toward her father's domineering manner and the double standard of gender dynamics that her father upholds. Like Amir and Baba, Soraya and her family are exiles from Afghanistan who assemble with the Afghan community at Saturday swap meets and other gatherings. Despite a scandalous past when she lived with a man to whom she was not married, Soraya endures the persistent gossip in the Afghan community and dedicates herself to the care of her new husband and father-in-law while pursing her goal of becoming a teacher.

Zaman

A struggling orphanage director in Kabul,

Zaman tells Amir and Farid where they can find the Taliban official who has abducted Sohrab.

THEMES

Identity and Self-Discovery

Throughout the novel, the protagonist struggles to find his true purpose and to forge an identity through noble actions. Amir's failure to stand by his friend at a crucial moment shapes this defining conflict. His endeavor to overcome his own weaknesses appears in his fear of Assef, his hesitation to enter a war-torn country ruled by the repressive Taliban, and even his carsickness while driving with Farid into Afghanistan. Late in the novel, Amir discovers his father's lifelong deception about his half brother Hassan, a revelation that leads to a deeper understanding of who his father was and how he and his father had both betrayed the people who were loyal to them.

Family, Fathers, and Fatherhood

In this novel in which family relationships play a great part, mothers are strikingly absent. Although Soraya is a loving mother to Sohrab, Amir and Hassan grow up without their mothers. Meanwhile, the tension of father-son relationships is exemplified by Baba's treatment of his sons, Amir and Hassan. While Baba is disappointed in Amir's bookish, introverted personality, to protect his social standing, he does not publicly acknowledge his illegitimate son Hassan whose mother is a

Hazara. Likewise, General Taheri is a traditional, highly critical father who chafes at his grown daughter's sometimes rebellious attitudes. The theme re-emerges in the marriage of Amir and Soraya, who try unsuccessfully to start a family of their own. Their adoption of the troubled and parentless Sohrab at the end of the novel marks an attempt to recreate a complete family based on relationships of love and honesty.

Journey and Quest

A novel of immigration and political unrest, *The Kite Runner* is punctuated by Amir's departure from Afghanistan as a teenager and his return to his war-ravaged home country as an adult. At the same time, it is a novel of symbolic quest. Amir makes great sacrifices to pursue his quest to atone for past sins by rescuing his half nephew. Symbolized by the bleeding fingers of kite-fighters who cut their competitors'kites out of the sky with string embedded with glass, sacrifice is an important theme of the novel. Near the beginning of the novel, Amir willingly cut his fingers to impress his father with a kite-fighting victory; at the end he cuts his fingers flying a kite to revive his spiritually wounded nephew from a profound depression. Whereas the young Amir compares Hassan's resignation to his attackers'assault to the resignation of a sacrificed animal, by the end of the novel, Amir is prepared to sacrifice much in order to save Hassan's son from a similar fate.

Heritage and Ancestry

Before leaving Afghanistan, Baba fills a snuff box with soil from his homeland. As refugees in the United States, Baba and Amir live in an Afghan immigrant community in the San Francisco Bay Area. Even though much of the action takes place in the United States, most of the characters there are Afghan, emphasizing how Amir and Baba thrive in and contribute to an immigrant community that reminds them of home. Although Baba dies without ever seeing his home country again, Amir maintains his ties to the Afghan community in Northern California, partly through his wife's family. Descriptions of Amir and Soraya's courtship and Baba's funeral exemplify such ties to traditional cultural values. The reader is treated to detailed accounts of the *khastegari* tradition in which the groom's father requests permission of the prospective bride's father, and the elaborate traditional ceremony in which Amir and Soraya are married. Although Amir first views living in the United States as a way to forget a painful past, he maintains and revives his ties to Afghan culture and religion. He returns to his country of birth and, after his nephew attempts suicide, re-discovers Islam as a source of strength. The narration and dialogue welcome the reader into this ethnic Pashtun and Afghan national identity through running translations of frequently spoken or culturally significant phrases and concepts.

MEDIA ADAPTATIONS

- What would have happened if Amir had fought to rescue Hassan from Assef, instead of running away? Would Hassan and Ali have moved with Baba and Amir to California? How would the boys'lives have been different? Create a timeline of events and milestones for each boy as their lives were presented in the novel, then create a new timeline for each boy to reflect how his life might have changed if Amir had saved Hassan.

- Return to the middle chapters of the novel, when Amir's wife Soraya interacts with her father and mother. Think about the ways that traditional Afghan culture, as Hosseini represents it in the novel, appears to have differing expectations of men and women. How have Soraya Taheri and her mother Khanum Taheri been affected by the ways that women's behavior is constrained by traditional Afghan culture? Write a two-page essay in which you discuss how the politics of gender in Afghan culture affects the characters in the novel, using concrete examples from the book to support your arguments.

- Gather in a small group and study the scene from pages 70 to 79. Then review the confrontation between Amir and Assef in Chapter 22. How has Amir changed in the years between the early scene and the later one? Next, think about the letter from Hassan that Rahim Khan presents to Amir. Suppose Amir wrote a letter in response. As a group, write a one-page letter in which Amir explains to Hassan how his character, goals, or understanding of the world has changed. Provide specific details from the novel to support Amir's claims.

- Think about Amir's relationship with Baba as it is detailed in Chapter 2 through Chapter 7. Make a list of the adjectives that describe Amir. Now make a list of adjectives that describe Baba. How are Baba and Amir alike? How are they different? In a short essay, describe the relationship between Baba and Amir, giving at least four concrete examples from the novel to support your points.

- Twice in the novel, the character Assef is associated with Adolf Hitler. Research the early twentieth-century German nationalist movement that led to Nazism. Based on the novel's depiction of the Taliban regime, make a list comparing and contrasting how citizens responded to the two regimes. How did Nazism affect Germany from the 1930s to the 1940s? How were the effects of the Taliban regime in Afghanistan from the mid-1990s to the early 2000s similar or different? Include specific examples from the novel to support your arguments.

Assimilation and Acculturation

From the early twentieth century to

contemporary times, new arrivals to the United States have lived and worked in their new homeland, attempting to lead better lives and simultaneously struggling to adjust to a culture that may or may not accept their traditions. When Amir and Baba arrive in Fremont, California, they, too, must start new lives. While Baba works at a humble job in a service station, Amir attends school, graduating from high school at the age of twenty. While Baba (like General Taheri, a man of his generation) dreams of returning to Afghanistan in better times, Amir who has spent much of his teenage years in the United States, adjusts more readily to his new country. For Amir, as for many in the literature of the American immigrant experience, the United States represents a space for new beginnings and a way to erase a dark, violent past. For Baba, the transition is more difficult, and his new life presents a painful contrast with his former position of power and prestige in Kabul.

Political Power/Abuse of Power

The events of the novel occur against the backdrop of political change, culminating in the rise of the tyrannical Taliban government in contemporary Afghanistan. Assef, Hassan's rapist and the bully who becomes a high-ranking Taliban official, embodies the consequences of the abuse of power for power's sake and the violence and repression of the Taliban regime. Assef is a sociopath who thrives in an atmosphere of chaos and subjugation. Interpersonal violence leads to the split between Amir and Hassan; on a national scale, the abuse of power by the Soviet-backed Communist regime in Afghanistan forces Baba and Amir to go into exile. The abuse of political and social power also appears in frequent references to the Hazara people, who are second-class citizens in the quasi-caste system of Afghanistan. At the beginning of the novel, Hazara characters such as Hassan's father Ali suffer public humiliation for their appearance. When General Taheri demands an explanation for Amir and Soraya's adoption of a Sohrab, "a Hazara boy," he echoes the discrimination against this entire ethnic minority. Likewise, he gives voice to this attitude when he attacks Amir for having a Hazara boy for a playmate. In a sense, even Baba condones systematic discrimination against Hazara people by refusing to acknowledge his son with a Hazara woman, Sanaubar.

STYLE

Flashback and Foreshadowing

Khaled Hosseini frequently uses flashback and foreshadowing. Indeed, most of the novel, which begins in 2001 and ends in 2002, is an elaborate flashback that brings the reader from the narrator's childhood to his young adulthood to his manhood. Within this overarching structure, Hosseini's use of time devices provide the reader and the narrator with information about what has happened outside the action of the novel so far, as in Chapter 16, in which Rahim Khan updates Amir on what has happened to Hassan since Amir and Baba left Kabul, or in Hassan's letter, in which some of the same events are told from a different point of view.

The use of time devices like foreshadowing may also prepare the reader for an imminent event or crisis. For example, during a description of Hassan's face in Chapter 7, the narrator breaks into the description to tell the reader that this was the last time he would see Hassan's smile except in a photograph, an interruption of the forward narrative that warns the reader that something momentous is in the offing. Sometimes the use of these techniques appears to signal moments when the lives of individuals are changed forever by violence, death, or the consequences of world events. One example occurs in Chapter 22, when Amir, seated in the house of the Taliban official, nervously eats a grape from a bowl on the table. Amir remarks, "The grape was sweet. I popped another one in [my mouth], unaware that it would be the last bit of solid food I would eat for a long time," thus preparing the reader for the violence of the imminent confrontation between Amir and Assef. Foreshadowing also plays a part in Chapter 7 when Amir witnesses the attack on Hassan on the night of his victory in the kite tournament:

> I had one last chance to make a decision. One final opportunity to decide who I was going to be. I could step into that alley, stand up for Hassan—the way he'd stood up for me all those times in the past— and accept whatever would happen to me. Or I could run.

This internal monologue hints that in the future Amir will suffer from a crisis in identity. Later in the novel, his failure to stand up for Hassan in his moment of need becomes a burden he carries for much of his life, and forces Amir to take drastic measures to recover his sense of himself as a good person.

Diction

The dialogue, or quoted conversation between characters, and the narration use a variety of modes to affect the reader. The diction ranges from detailed description to conversational. One feature of the novel's use of language is its frequent references to Afghan culture and its use of terms from Pashtu and Farsi that denote important concepts in Afghan tradition and in the lives of the Afghan community in the San Francisco Bay Area. Such terms are nearly always translated for non-Pashtu- and non-Farsi-speaking readers in a way that invites the reader to become familiar with Afghan culture while remaining engaged in the flow of action. The writing is peppered with words in Farsi and Dari (which is the version of Farsi commonly spoken in Afghanistan), followed by brief translations set off by commas. In addition to the oftheard greeting *Salaam Aleikum* and the oath *inshallah*, the reader learns the meanings of such expressions as *ihtiram* (respect); *nazar* (the evil eye); *lotfan* (please); *yateem* (orphans); and *zendagi migzara* (life goes on). For example, when Amir asks his father to ask Soraya's father for permission for Amir and Soraya to marry, in accordance with Afghan tradition, he says, "I want you to go *khastegari*. I want you to ask General Taheri for his daughter's hand." Similarly, when Soraya tells Amir about a secret from her past, he thinks, "I couldn't lie to her and say that my pride, my *iftikhar*, wasn't stung at all."

Interior Monologue

Interior monologue, or the words a character uses to describe his or her own feelings to him-or herself, is an important technique through which Hosseini enables the reader to become acquainted with the narrator Amir, and through him, the Afghan culture and history that propel much of the action of the story. Internal monologue is a particularly important device in this work because the action is as much propelled by political developments as by the protagonist's psychological development.

Imagery and Symbolism

The novel invites the reader to view images and symbols in the first part of the novel as mirrored by those at the end. For example, the novel is book-ended by two kite contests. The imagery of kite-fighting dominates the scene that marks the last happy moments Hassan and Amir enjoy together. At the end of the novel, a smaller kite contest between the adult Amir and a young Afghan American boy, as Sohrab looks on, suggests redemption for Amir, who has never forgiven himself for what happened to Hassan on the night of that first kite-fighting contest in Kabul years before. Similarly, Assef's attack on Hassan as the twelve-year-old Amir looks on is echoed in the battle between the adult Amir and Assef late in the novel

HISTORICAL CONTEXT

The Kite Runner, set in Afghanistan and the United States from the 1970s to 2002, presents a story of intertwined personal conflicts and tragedies against a historical background of national and cultural trauma. The early chapters tell much about the richness of Afghan culture as experienced by the young Amir and Hassan in the Afghan capital, Kabul. The novel's account of the culture of Kabul informs the reader about everything from the melon sellers in the bazaar to the cosmopolitan social and intellectual lives of Kabul elite society during the monarchy, to the traditional pastimes of Afghan children. Detailed descriptions treat the reader to such events as a large extended-family outing to a lake and the annual winter kite tournament of Kabul. Subsequent political developments, however, appear to curtail these relative freedoms, as first the Soviet-backed Communist government, then the Northern Alliance, and finally the Taliban progressively repress the activities of Afghan citizens. The reader learns the effects of the first of these developments through first-person narration; the effects of the Northern Alliance and of Taliban rule emerge in Rahim Khan's, Farid's, and Hassan's accounts of Afghan life in the period between the late 1980s and the early 2000s. Starting in the early chapters of the novel, broad political events such as the revolution that overthrows the monarchy come to form not just a background for the action, but to become prime movers of the plot. The sound of gunfire in Chapter 5, for example, initiates a series of political shake-ups that eventually leads to the Communist takeover of Afghanistan and drives Baba and Amir, along with many of the privileged class, into exile. In addition, it marks an end to a period that was—despite being marred by the iniquities of the caste system—relatively idyllic. As Amir observes, "The generation of Afghan children whose ears would know nothing but the sounds of bombs and gunfire was not yet born." This observation foreshadows the traumatized condition of Amir's nephew Sohrab, born in the midst of violence and orphaned and abused by the Taliban.

The Kite Runner is one of the first works of fiction to include the September 11, 2001 attacks on the United States within the span of its narrative. In the aftermath of the September 11 attacks, Afghanistan was portrayed in popular media as a country whose government allowed a terrorist organization to operate within its borders and committed human rights abuses against its own people. Through a detailed personal narrative, the novel re-focuses attention on Afghanistan through a different lens, correcting this narrow view of a country which, despite its problems, has a fascinating history.

Another important historical and cultural context of the novel is the diverse and variegated world of contemporary multicultural America, particularly in California. Hosseini, the son of a diplomat and a teacher, left Afghanistan with his family in 1981, much like Amir. Likewise, Amir's experiences in the Afghan immigrant community of Fremont, California, familiarly known in the San Francisco Bay Area as "Little Kabul," may reflect the author's experiences of the area from arrival in San Jose in the 1980s. Amir's life as a young immigrant in the multicultural space of the Bay Area illustrates the increased mixing of diverse ethnicities in the 1980s and 1990s within U.S. popular culture.

The novel also gives a detailed account of how one ethnic group formed a cultural enclave within American culture so that its members could help one another and preserve Afghan cultural traditions. Detailed descriptions in the middle and late chapters give the reader a window on some cultural practices, both formal and informal, that help define the Afghan community in Fremont. Amir's and Soraya's lives are certainly taken up with the broader American culture. Both attend public schools and (we presume) mix with non-Afghan students; Amir takes creative writing classes in which he must read about the experiences of a diverse group of young writers; and Soraya has a career as a writing instructor at a community college. Still their identities as Afghans or Afghan Americans are defined in part by the ceremonies and practices of their families and their community. The Saturday swap meets, for example, exemplify the well-documented strategy of immigrant groups to adapt already existing institutions in the United States as ways to preserve their cultures of origin.

CRITICAL OVERVIEW

The Kite Runner was published in 2003 to nearly unanimous praise. Said to be the first novel written in English by an Afghan, the novel was instantly popular. Its first printing was fifty thousand copies, it has been featured on the reading lists of countless book clubs, and foreign rights to the novel have been sold in at least ten countries.

Reviewers admired the novel for its straightforward storytelling, its convincing character studies, and for its startling account of the human toll of the violence that has accompanied Afghanistan's turbulent political scene in the last thirty years. In his review in *World Literature Today*, Ronny Noor remarks, "This lucidly written and often touching novel gives a vivid picture of not only the Russian atrocities but also those of the Northern Alliance and the Taliban." A brief review in *Publishers Weekly* credited the novel with providing "an incisive, perceptive examination of recent Afghan history and its ramifications in both America and the Middle East," and called it "a complete work of literature that succeeds in exploring the culture of a previously obscure nation that has become a pivot point in the global politics of the new millennium." The novel was noted for its detailed portrayal of a friendship between two boys that tenuously spans class and ethnic lines. In the *New York Times Book Review*, Edward Hower praises the novel for its detailed descriptions of life in Kabul in the 1970s: "Hosseini's depiction of pre-revolutionary Afghanistan is rich in warmth and humor but also tense with the friction of different ethnic groups." Hower also notes how the class distinctions between Amir and Hassan make their relationship all the more vulnerable: "Amir is served breakfast every morning by Hassan; then he is driven to school in a shiny Mustang while his friend stays home to clean the house."

A few noted with misgiving that the novel occasionally strays from the conventions of realism in contemporary fiction. Hower notes, "When Amir meets his old nemesis, now a powerful Taliban official, the book descends into some plot twists better suited to a folk tale than a modern novel." Like Hower, Rebecca Stuhr of the *Library Journal* focuses on the late chapters in pointing out the novel's "over-reliance on coincidence." In an otherwise glowing review in the *Times Literary Supplement*, James O'Brien points out that "When Hosseini strays from the simple narrative style he prefers, he struggles to retain credibility." Noor argued that the novel gives "a selective, simplistic, even simple-minded picture" of the ongoing Afghan conflict, in particular an overly optimistic view of Hamid Karzai's ability to govern Afghanistan. Overall, reviewers see the novel as a great triumph marred only by rare stylistic flaws.

SOURCES

Hosseini, Khaled, *The Kite Runner*, Riverhead Books, 2003.

Hower, Edward, "The Servant," in the *New York Times Book Review*, August 3, 2003, p. 4.

Katsoulis, Melissa, "Kites of Passage" in the *Times* (London), August 30, 2003, Features section, p. 17.

Noor, Ronny, Review of *The Kite Runner*, in *World Literature Today*, Vol. 78, Nos. 3-4, September-December 2004, p. 148.

O'Brien, James, "The Sins of the Father," in the *Times Literary Supplement*, October 10, 2003, p. 25.

Review of *The Kite Runner*, in *Publishers Weekly*, Vol. 250, No. 19, May 12, 2003, p. 43.

Stuhr, Rebecca, Review of *The Kite Runner*, in *Library Journal*, April 15, 2003, p. 122.

Hosseini, Khaled, *Dreaming in Titanic City*, Riverhead Books.

> This follow-up to Hosseini's extremely successful first novel is set to be published in 2006.

FURTHER READING

Lipson, J. G., and P. A. Omidian, "Afghan Refugee Issues in the U.S. Social Environment" in *Western Journal of Nursing Research*, Vol. 19, No. 1, February 1997, pp. 110-26.

> The article focuses on the physical and mental health challenges faced by Afghan refugees since they began to arrive in the San Francisco Bay Area in the 1980s. Based on an ethnographic study and using quotations from interviews with these newcomers, the article examines stresses caused by the new social contexts within which Afghan refugees find themselves and how they perceive their interactions with American citizens and institutions.

Ondaatje, Michael, *Anil's Ghost*, Vintage Books, 2000.

> In Ondaadtje's fifth novel, the protagonist Anil Tessera is a Sri Lankan forensic anthropologist educated in England and the United States, who returns to work in Sri Lanka. In the course of uncovering gruesome evidence of violence wrought by the civil war there, she re-connects with centuries of Sri

Lankan tradition and is confronted with the senseless destruction brought about by interethnic conflict in the country of her birth.

Payant, Katherine B., and Toby Rose, eds., *The Immigrant Experience in North American Literature: Carving Out a Niche*, 2003.

This book contains a collection of essays by various scholars who discuss the ways that North American literature has represented the experiences of immigrant groups entering and becoming acculturated to the United States. Essays include discussions of such authors as Anzia Yezierska to Jamaica Kincaid.

Rashid, Ahmed, *Taliban: Militant Islam, Oil and Fundamentalism in Central Asia*, Yale University Press, 2000.

Ahmed, a journalist in Afghanistan for over twenty years, sketches the Taliban's rise to power between 1994 to 1999, as well as other countries'attempts to gain control over the development of Afghanistan. His account discusses the Taliban's ideological foundations, its well-known repression of women, and its ties to the heroin trade.

Lightning Source UK Ltd.
Milton Keynes UK
UKHW02f0230150518
322586UK00005B/496/P